Rubáiyát
of Omar
Khayyám.

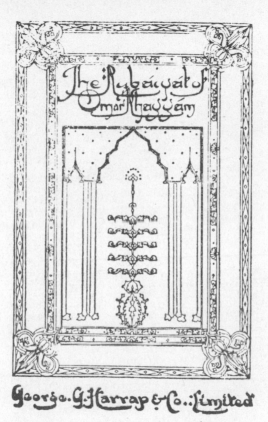

The Rubáiyát of Omar Khayyám

George G. Harrap & Co., Limited

The illustrations and decorations in this edition of FitzGerald's
translation of the "Rubaiyat" are by WILLY POGANY

First published in Great Britain October 1916
by GEORGE G. HARRAP & CO. LTD.
182 High Holborn, London WC1V 7AX

Reprinted: 1917 (*twice*); 1918; 1919 (*twice*); 1920;
1923; 1924; 1925; 1927; 1928; 1931; 1934; 1935;
1938; 1940; 1942; 1944; 1946; 1949; 1951; 1954;
1957; 1961; 1965; 1971; 1976; 1979

ISBN 0 245 57460 3

Text Printed in Great Britain by
Biddles Ltd, Guildford, Surrey
Colour Printed in Great Britain by
Pinepoint Ltd, London

THE RUBÁIYÁT

AWAKE! for Morning in the
Bowl of Night
Has flung the Stone that puts the
Stars to Flight:
And Lo! the Hunter of the East
has caught
The Sultán's Turret in a Noose of
Light.

DREAMING when Dawn's Left
  Hand was in the Sky,
I heard a Voice within the Tavern
  cry,
 "Awake, my Little ones, and fill
  the Cup
Before Life's Liquor in its Cup be
  dry."

A ND as the Cock crew, those who
stood before
The Tavern shouted—"Open then
the Door!
You know how little while we
have to stay,
And, once departed, may return no
more."

NOW the New Year reviving old
  Desires,
The thoughtful Soul to Solitude
  retires,
  Where the WHITE HAND OF MOSES
  on the Bough
Puts out, and Jesus from the Ground
  suspires.

IRÁM indeed is gone with all its
   Rose,
And Jamshýd's Sev'n-ring'd Cup
   where no one knows;
  But still the Vine her ancient Ruby
   yields,
And still a Garden by the Water
   blows.

A ND David's Lips are lock't; but
in divine
High-piping Péhlevi, with "Wine!
Wine! Wine!
Red Wine!"—the Nightingale cries
to the Rose
That yellow Cheek of hers t'incar-
nadine.

COME, fill the Cup, and in the
    Fire of Spring
The Winter Garment of Repentance
    fling :
  The Bird of Time has but a little
    way
To fly—and Lo! the Bird is on the
    Wing.

AND look—a thousand Blossoms
with the Day
Woke—and a thousand scatter'd into
Clay:
And this first Summer Month that
brings the Rose
Shall take Jamshýd and Kaikobád
away.

BUT come with old Khayyám and
    leave the Lot
Of Kaikobád and Kaikhosru forgot:
    Let Rustum lay about him as he
    will,
Or Hátim Tai cry Supper—heed them
    not.

WITH me along some strip of Herbage strown
That just divides the desert from the sown,
  Where name of Slave and Sultán scarce is known,
And pity Sultán Máhmúd on his Throne.

HERE with a Loaf of Bread beneath the Bough,
A Flask of Wine, a Book of Verse—
    and Thou
  Beside me singing in the Wilderness—
    ness—
And Wilderness is Paradise enow.

"HOW sweet is mortal Sovranty!"
—think some:
Others—"How blest the Paradise to
come!"
  Ah, take the Cash in hand and
  waive the Rest;
Oh, the brave Music of a *distant*
Drum!

L OOK to the Rose that blows about us—"Lo,
Laughing," she says, "into the World I blow:
  At once the silken Tassel of my Purse
Tear, and its Treasure on the Garden throw."

THE Worldly Hope men set their
  Hearts upon
Turns Ashes—or it prospers; and
  anon,
  Like Snow upon the Desert's dusty
  Face
Lighting a little Hour or two—is
  gone.

AND those who husbanded the
Golden Grain,
And those who flung it to the Winds
like Rain,
Alike to no such aureate Earth are
turn'd
As, buried once, Men want dug up
again.

THINK, in this batter'd Cara-
vanserai
Whose Doorways are alternate Night
and Day,
How Sultán after Sultán with his
Pomp
Abode his Hour or two, and went
his way.

THEY say the Lion and the
    Lizard keep
The Courts where Jamshýd gloried
    and drank deep:
    And Bahrám, that great Hunter—
    the Wild Ass
Stamps o'er his Head, and he lies
    fast asleep.

I SOMETIMES think that never
blows so red
The Rose as where some buried
Cæsar bled;
That every Hyacinth the Garden
wears
Dropt in its Lap from some once
lovely Head.

A ND this delightful Herb whose
tender Green
Fledges the River's Lip on which we
lean—
Ah, lean upon it lightly! for who
knows
From what once Lovely Lip it springs
unseen!

AH, my Belovéd, fill the cup that
    clears
TO-DAY of past Regrets and future
    Fears—
  To-morrow?—Why, To-morrow I
    may be
Myself with Yesterday's Sev'n Thou-
    sand Years.

L O! some we loved, the loveliest
   and the best
That Time and Fate of all their
   Vintage prest,
  Have drunk their Cup a Round or
   two before,
And one by one crept silently to
   Rest.

A ND we, that now make merry
in the Room
They left, and Summer dresses in
new Bloom,
  Ourselves must we beneath the
  Couch of Earth
Descend, ourselves to make a Couch
—for whom?

A H, make the most of what we
yet may spend,
Before we too into the Dust descend;
  Dust into Dust, and under Dust,
  to lie,
Sans Wine, sans Song, sans Singer,
  and—sans End!

A LIKE for those who for TO-DAY
prepare,
And those that after a TO-MORROW
stare,
A Muezzín from the Tower of
Darkness cries,
"Fools! your Reward is neither Here
nor There!"

WHY, all the Saints and Sages
    who discuss'd
Of the Two worlds so learnedly, are
    thrust
  Like foolish Prophets forth; their
    Words to Scorn
Are scatter'd, and their Mouths are
    stopt with Dust.

OH, come with old Khayyám, and
   leave the Wise
To talk; one thing is certain, that
   Life flies;
 One thing is certain, and the Rest
   is Lies;
The Flower that once has blown for
   ever dies.

MYSELF when young did eagerly
    frequent
Doctor and Saint, and heard great
    Argument
  About it and about: but evermore
Came out by the same Door as in I
    went.

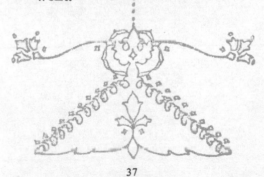

WITH them the Seed of Wisdom
     did I sow,
And with my own hand labour'd it
     to grow:
  And this was all the Harvest that
     I reap'd—
"I came like Water, and like Wind
     I go."

INTO this Universe, and *why* not
   knowing,
Nor *whence*, like Water willy-nilly
   flowing!
  And out of it, as Wind along the
   Waste,
I know not *whither*, willy-nilly
   blowing.

WHAT, without asking, hither hurried *whence*?
And, without asking, *whither* hurried hence!
Another and another Cup to drown
The Memory of this Impertinence!

UP from Earth's Centre through
   the Seventh Gate
I rose, and on the Throne of Saturn
   sate,
   And many Knots unravel'd by
    the Road;
But not the Knot of Human Death
   and Fate.

THERE was a Door to which I
found no Key:
There was a Veil past which I could
not see:
Some little Talk awhile of ME and
THEE
There seem'd—and then no more of
THEE and ME.

THEN to the rolling Heav'n itself
    I cried,
Asking, "What Lamp had Destiny to
    guide
  Her little Children stumbling in
    the Dark?"
And—"A blind Understanding!"
    Heav'n replied.

45

THEN to this earthen Bowl did I
adjourn
My Lip the secret Well of Life to
learn:
And Lip to Lip it murmur'd—
"While you live
Drink!—for once dead you never
shall return."

I THINK the Vessel, that with fugitive
Articulation answer'd, once did live,
  And merry-make; and the cold
  Lip I kiss'd
How many Kisses might it take—and
  give!

F OR in the Market-place, one
    Dusk of Day,
I watch'd the Potter thumping his
    wet Clay:
    And with its all obliterated Tongue
It murmur'd — "Gently, Brother,
    gently, pray!"

A H, fill the Cup:—what boots it
to repeat
How time is slipping underneath our
Feet:
Unborn TO-MORROW and dead
YESTERDAY,
Why fret about them if TO-DAY be
sweet!

ONE Moment in Annihilation's
    Waste,
One Moment, of the Well of Life to
    taste—
  The Stars are setting and the
    Caravan
Starts for the Dawn of Nothing
    —Oh, make haste!

HOW long, how long, in infinite
    Pursuit
Of This and That endeavour and
    dispute?
  Better be merry with the fruitful
    Grape
Than sadden after none, or bitter,
    Fruit.

YOU know, my Friends, how long
    since in my House
For a new Marriage I did make
    Carouse:
    Divorced old barren Reason from
    my Bed,
And took the Daughter of the Vine
    to Spouse.

F OR "Is" and "Is-not" though
  with Rule and Line,
And "Up-and-down" *without*, I could
  define,
  I yet in all I only cared to know,
Was never deep in anything but
  —Wine.

A ND lately, by the Tavern Door
      agape,
Came stealing through the Dusk an
    Angel Shape
    Bearing a Vessel on his Shoulder;
      and
He bid me taste of it; and 'twas—the
    Grape!

THE Grape that can with Logic
    absolute
The Two-and-Seventy jarring Sects
    confute:
  The subtle Alchemist that in a
    Trice
Life's leaden Metal into Gold trans-
    mute.

THE mighty Mahmúd, the victorious Lord,
That all the misbelieving and black
   Horde
   Of Fears and Sorrows that infest
   the Soul
Scatters and slays with his enchanted
   Sword.

BUT leave the Wise to wrangle,
    and with me
The Quarrel of the Universe let be:
    And, in some corner of the Hubbub
    coucht,
Make Game of that which makes as
    much of Thee.

FOR in and out, above, about,
    below,
'Tis nothing but a Magic Shadow-
    show,
  Play'd in a Box whose Candle is
    the Sun,
Round which we Phantom Figures
    come and go.

AND if the Wine you drink, the
Lip you press,
End in the Nothing all Things end
in—Yes—
Then fancy while Thou art, Thou
art but what
Thou shalt be—Nothing—Thou shalt
not be less.

WHILE the Rose blows along the
River Brink,
With old Khayyám the Ruby Vint-
age drink:
And when the Angel with his
darker Draught
Draws up to Thee—take that, and do
not shrink.

'TIS all a Chequer-board of Nights
and Days
Where Destiny with Men for Pieces
plays:
Hither and thither moves, and
mates, and slays,
And one by one back in the Closet
lays.

THE Ball no Question makes of
　　Ayes and Noes,
But Right or Left as strikes the
　　Player goes;
　And He that toss'd Thee down into
　　the Field,
He knows about it all—He knows—
　　HE knows!

THE Moving Finger writes; and,
    having writ,
Moves on: nor all thy Piety nor Wit
    Shall lure it back to cancel half a
    Line,
Nor all thy Tears wash out a Word
    of it.

A ND that inverted Bowl we call
      The Sky,
Whereunder crawling coop't we live
      and die,
   Lift not thy hands to *It* for help—
      for It
Rolls impotently on as Thou or I.

WITH Earth's first Clay They did
    the Last Man's knead,
And then of the Last Harvest sow'd
    the Seed :
    Yea, the first Morning of Creation
    wrote
What the Last Dawn of Reckoning
    shall read.

I TELL Thee this—When, starting
   from the Goal,
Over the shoulders of the flaming
   Foal
  Of Heav'n Parwín and Mushtara
   they flung,
In my predestin'd Plot of Dust and
   Soul

THE Vine had struck a Fibre; which about
  If clings my being—let the Súfi flout;
    Of my Base Metal may be filed a Key,
That shall unlock the Door he howls without.

A ND this I know: whether the
  one True Light,
Kindle to Love, or Wrath consume
    me quite,
  One glimpse of It within the
    Tavern caught
Better than in the Temple lost out-
    right.

OH Thou, who didst with Pitfall
and with Gin
Beset the Road I was to wander in,
   Thou wilt not with Predestination
   round
Enmesh me, and impute my Fall to
   Sin?

OH Thou, who Man of baser Earth
      didst make,
And who with Eden didst devise the
      Snake;
   For all the Sin wherewith the Face
      of man
Is blacken'd, Man's Forgiveness give
      —and take!

KÚZA—NÁMA

L ISTEN again. One evening at
the Close
Of Ramazán, ere the better Moon
arose,
In that old Potter's Shop I stood
alone
With the clay Population round in
Rows.

A ND, strange to tell, among that
Earthen Lot
Some could articulate, while others
not:
And suddenly one more impatient
cried—
"Who *is* the Potter, pray, and who
the Pot?"

T HEN said another—"Surely not
    in vain
My Substance from the common
    Earth was ta'en;
   That He who subtly wrought me
    into Shape
Should stamp me back to common
    Earth again."

A NOTHER said—"Why, ne'er a peevish Boy
Would break the Bowl from which he drank in Joy;
  Shall He that *made* the Vessel in pure Love
And Fancy, in an after Rage destroy!"

NONE answer'd this; but after Silence spake
A Vessel of a more ungainly Make:
  "They sneer at me for leaning all
    awry;
What! did the Hand then of the
    Potter shake?"

SAID one—"Folks of a surly Tap-
    ster tell,
And daub his Visage with the Smoke
    of Hell;
    They talk of some strict Testing of
      us—Pish!
He's a Good Fellow and 'twill all be
    well."

THEN said another with a long-
drawn Sigh,
"My Clay with long Oblivion is gone
dry:
But, fill me with the old familiar
Juice,
Methinks I might recover by-and-
bye!"

So while the Vessels one by one
    were speaking,
One spied the little Crescent all were
    seeking:
  And then they jogged each other,
  "Brother! Brother!
Hark to the Porter's Shoulder-knot
    a-creaking!"

AH, with the Grape my fading
Life provide,
And wash my Body whence the Life
has died,
And in a Windingsheet of Vine-
leaf wrapt,
So bury me by some sweet Garden-
side.

Tʜᴀᴛ ev'n my buried Ashes such
  a Snare
Of Perfume shall fling up into the
  Air,
  As not a True Believer passing by
But shall be overtaken unaware.

INDEED the Idols I have loved so
  long
Have done my Credit in Men's Eye
  much wrong:
  Have drown'd my Honour in a
  shallow Cup,
And sold my Reputation for a Song.

INDEED, indeed, Repentance oft
   before
I swore—but was I sober when I
   swore?
  And then and then came Spring,
    and Rose-in-hand
My thread-bare Penitence apieces
   tore.

A ND much as Wine has play'd the
Infidel,
And robb'd me of my Robe of Honour
—well,
I often wonder what the Vintners
buy
One half so precious as the Goods
they sell.

A LAS! that Spring should vanish
with the Rose!
That Youth's sweet-scented Manu-
script should close!
The Nightingale that in the
Branches sang,
Ah, whence, and whither flown again,
who knows!

AH, Love! could thou and I with Fate conspire
To grasp this sorry Scheme of Things entire,
  Would not we shatter it to bits—and then
Re-mould it nearer to the Heart's Desire!

AH, Moon of my Delight who
know'st no wane,
The Moon of Heaven is rising once
again:
How oft hereafter rising shall she
look
Through this same Garden after me
—in vain!

AND when Thyself with shining
Foot shall pass
Among the Guests Star-scatter'd on
the Grass
And in thy joyous Errand reach
the Spot
Where I made one—turn down an
empty Glass!

TAMÁM SHUD